W9-AOE-356

JOHN CENA:
HUSTLE. LOYALTY. RESPECT.

TEDDY BORTH

abdopublishing.com

Published by Abdo Zoom, a division of ABDO, P.O. Box 398166, Minneapolis, Minnesota 55439. Copyright © 2018 by Abdo Consulting Group, Inc. International copyrights reserved in all countries. No part of this book may be reproduced in any form without written permission from the publisher.

Printed in the United States of America, North Mankato, Minnesota.
092017
012018

THIS BOOK CONTAINS
RECYCLED MATERIALS

Photo Credits: Alamy, AllWrestlingSuperstars.com, AP Images, Icon Sportswire, iStock, newscom, Shutterstock, Seth Poppel/Yearbook Library
Production Contributors: Kenny Abdo, Jennie Forsberg, Grace Hansen
Design Contributors: Dorothy Toth, Neil Klinepier

Publisher's Cataloging-in-Publication Data

Names: Borth, Teddy, author.
Title: John Cena: hustle. loyalty. respect. / by Teddy Borth.
Other titles: Hustle. loyalty. respect.
Description: Minneapolis, Minnesota: Abdo Zoom, 2018. | Series: Wrestling biographies | Includes online resource and index.
Identifiers: LCCN 2017939287 | ISBN 9781532121098 (lib.bdg.)
    ISBN 9781532122217 (ebook) | ISBN 9781532122774 (Read-to-Me ebook)
Subjects: LCSH: Cena, John d1977- --Juvenile literature.
    Wrestlers--Juvenile literature. | Biography—Juvenile literature.
Classification: DDC 796.812 [B]--dc23
LC record available at https://lccn.loc.gov/2017939287

TABLE OF CONTENTS

EARLY LIFE

John Cena was born on
April 23, 1977. He was born in
West Newbury, Massachusetts.

Cena moved to California in 1998 to be a body builder. One year later, he tried wrestling.

ULTIMATE PRO WRESTLING

Cena joined Ultimate Pro Wrestling (UPW). He wrestled with the name The Prototype. Cena said that he was "50% man, 50% machine, and 100% mayhem."

On April 27, 2000, Cena became UPW Champion. By 2001, WWE called Cena to join Ohio Valley Wrestling (OVW).

OHIO VALLEY WRESTLING

OVW was a place to help wrestlers grow before going on TV. Cena won both the **Heavyweight title** and the **Tag Team** title there.

13

WWE TELEVISION DEBUT

On June 27, 2002, Cena made his WWE TV **debut**. He wrestled Kurt Angle. Cena lost the **match**, but he impressed many people.

CHAMPIONSHIPS

March 14, 2004, was **Wrestlemania** 20. Cena won his very first WWE **title** there. He beat The Big Show to become U.S. Champion.

18

At **Wrestlemania** 21, Cena finally won WWE's top prize. He was the WWE Champion! Cena won this **title** 16 more times to tie the record!

Cena uses the catchphrase "Hustle. Loyalty. Respect." He works hard. He can be trusted. He respects any wrestler who gets in the ring with him.

GLOSSARY

catchphrase – a saying a wrestler will use often.

debut – to appear for the first time.

heavyweight – a division for larger athletes.

match – a competition in which wrestlers fight against each other.

tag team – a division made up of teams of two people. Wrestlers tag their partner to get in and out of the match.

title – the position of being the best in that division.

Wrestlemania – WWE's biggest event of the year.